FOCUS ON ENDANGERED SPECIES
ENDANGERED WHALES

by Clara MacCarald

BrightPoint Press

San Diego, CA

© 2024 BrightPoint Press
an imprint of ReferencePoint Press, Inc.
Printed in the United States

For more information, contact:
BrightPoint Press
PO Box 27779
San Diego, CA 92198
www.BrightPointPress.com

ALL RIGHTS RESERVED.

No part of this work covered by the copyright hereon may be reproduced or used in any form or by any means—graphic, electronic, or mechanical, including photocopying, recording, taping, web distribution, or information storage retrieval systems—without the written permission of the publisher.

LIBRARY OF CONGRESS CATALOGING-IN-PUBLICATION DATA

Names: MacCarald, Clara, 1979- author.
Title: Endangered whales / by Clara MacCarald.
Description: San Diego, CA: BrightPoint Press, [2024] | Series: Focus on endangered species | Includes bibliographical references and index. | Audience: Ages 13 | Audience: Grades 7-9
Identifiers: LCCN 2023008668 (print) | LCCN 2023008669 (eBook) | ISBN 9781678206505 (hardcover) | ISBN 9781678206512 (eBook)
Subjects: LCSH: Whales--Conservation--Juvenile literature. | Endangered species--Juvenile literature.
Classification: LCC QL737.C4 M33 2024 (print) | LCC QL737.C4 (eBook) | DDC 599.5168--dc23/eng/20230320
LC record available at https://lccn.loc.gov/2023008668
LC eBook record available at https://lccn.loc.gov/2023008669

CONTENTS

AT A GLANCE	**4**
INTRODUCTION A WHALE IN DANGER	**6**
CHAPTER ONE NORTH ATLANTIC RIGHT WHALES	**10**
CHAPTER TWO SEI WHALES	**22**
CHAPTER THREE BLUE WHALES	**34**
CHAPTER FOUR GRAY WHALES	**46**
Glossary	58
Source Notes	59
For Further Research	60
Index	62
Image Credits	63
About the Author	64

AT A GLANCE

- Excessive whale hunting led to major drops in whale populations. The International Whaling Commission banned all commercial whaling starting in 1985.

- North Atlantic right whales are among the most endangered whale species in the world. Ship strikes and fishing gear are their biggest threats.

- Some countries have banned boats from getting too close to North Atlantic right whales. This helps prevent ships from hitting the whales.

- Japan left the International Whaling Commission so its people could continue to hunt whales for profit. The sei whale is one species the country allows whalers to hunt.

- Commercial whaling is becoming less popular. It's expensive to do, and younger people have little demand for whale products. This may drive commercial whalers out of business.

- Blue whales mainly eat a type of crustacean called krill. Krill populations are declining due to human activity. If krill populations keep dropping, blue whales won't have enough to eat.

- Despite the threats facing blue whales, their populations are increasing. They're now found in every ocean except the Arctic Ocean.

- Gray whales live in two populations in the North Pacific. In the 1700s, they were hunted almost to the point of extinction.

- Gray whales are a popular species for whale watching. Whale watching can bother and harm the animals, but it can also help conservationists educate people about whales.

INTRODUCTION

A WHALE IN DANGER

A North Atlantic right whale swims off the coast of Georgia. This right whale is in trouble. Ropes wrap around the animal's middle. More ropes trail behind the whale.

The ropes had been connected to buoys. Crab trappers use buoys to find their traps and pull them out of the water. When the right whale swam by the ropes, it became caught in them.

A boat approaches the whale. The whale doesn't move away. It's too weak. Dragging the ropes for days has tired it out.

In 2018, there were more than 1 million fishing lines strewn throughout right whale habitats.

The people in the boat carefully steer closer. When they're close enough, they cut away the ropes.

The right whale swims free. It will rest, feed, and hopefully recover. The people in the boat have saved one of the few North Atlantic right whales left in the world.

WHALING WOES

People began whaling thousands of years ago. Whalers hunted the animals for meat, bones, and other parts. By the early 1900s, people were becoming concerned about falling whale populations. The International

More than 80 percent of right whales observed between 1980 and 2009 showed signs of having been tangled in fishing gear.

Whaling Commission (IWC) banned all **commercial** whaling starting in 1985. Some whale species have been able to recover since the ban. Others are still endangered.

1
NORTH ATLANTIC RIGHT WHALES

Right whales are broad and black. They have wide tails and short flippers. On their heads are rough patches of skin. Sea lice live on these patches and turn the skin white. The oldest right whales live for about sixty-five years. If not for human activities, they might be able to live longer.

Right whales are baleen whales. This means that they have baleen plates instead of teeth. Baleen plates are huge comblike plates on a whale's upper jaw. The plates are close together and act as strainers.

North Atlantic right whales can weigh up to 140,000 pounds (63,500 kg).

Some whales may stay tangled in fishing gear for years.

Right whales eat tiny **crustaceans** called copepods. To eat, whales scoop a huge amount of water into their mouths. Then they squeeze the water out. The baleen plates strain out copepods for the whales to swallow.

North Atlantic right whales have feeding grounds off the coasts of New England and Canada. Some of the whales **migrate** south for the winter. Females give birth to calves in waters near the southeastern United States.

WHALING AND FISHING GEAR

Right whales were once popular prey for whalers. The National Oceanic and Atmospheric Administration (NOAA) explains that the species "got their name from being the 'right' whales to hunt because they floated when they were killed."[1] This made it

A group of whales is called a pod. North Atlantic right whales sometimes migrate in small pods.

easier to harvest parts from the whales. By the 1890s, North Atlantic right whales were almost **extinct**.

In 1935, countries around the world agreed to ban the hunting of right whales. But North Atlantic right whales never fully recovered. In some years, the population increased. In others, numbers went down. The right whale population started shrinking again in 2010. Right whales were dying due to being struck by ships and caught in fishing gear.

Any size ship can hurt or kill a right whale. A ship strike can break the animal's bones. Propellers can make deep cuts in the whale's skin. The danger is worse if the ship is large or going fast.

Fishing gear is another big danger for right whales. Every year, about fifty right whales get caught in fishing gear. Fishing gear includes lines from lobster and crab traps. It also includes nets.

Fishing gear causes 58 percent of right whale deaths. Those that survive

WHALE OIL

Blubber is a thick layer of fat. Whale blubber keeps whales warm and helps them float. Whalers used to use right whale blubber to make whale oil. Whale oil can be used for many different things. People burned whale oil in lamps for light. They made whale oil into soap. The oil was even used to make leather and explosives.

sometimes drag the lines for miles. The lines can cut into their skin. The cuts and stress weaken the animals even once the gear is gone. Scientists suspect this may be causing females to have fewer calves.

Another big problem is noise. Over time, the number of ships and boats in right whale territory has increased. Humans also build along the coast. All this activity is very loud. The noise can make it hard for the whales to hear each other. The animals can also have trouble hearing ships or predators.

SAVING RIGHT WHALES

There are many **conservation** efforts underway to save North Atlantic right whales. One way to protect the whales is by reducing the chance of ship strikes. The US government has moved shipping lanes away from places where right whales gather. Shipping lanes are the paths boats take to get from one place to another. By US law, ships must stay 500 yards (457 m) from right whales. Large boats must slow down in certain areas. Speed limits can greatly lower the number of right whales hit.

Scientists have also found ways to alert ships to the presence of whales. For example, some buoys have devices that listen for whale calls. When a buoy hears a right whale, scientists let ships in the area know. The ships can then slow down and look out for the creatures. Scientists have

WHALE SOUNDS

Whales make many different noises. Right whale noises can sound like a groan or a gunshot. Some whale species sing. These species include blue whales and fin whales. Humpback whales are famous for their long, structured songs. Most right whales don't sing. But scientists recorded some North Pacific right whales singing in 2017.

also created an online map that shows the locations of recent right whale sightings.

Some conservationists work to free whales caught in fishing gear. Others design tools to prevent whales from getting caught altogether. For example, some traps have ropes that are designed to easily break to allow tangled whales to escape. Other traps don't use rope at all. When it's time to check the trap, a device blows up a balloon. The trap then floats to the surface.

In 2021, there were only 340 North Atlantic right whales left on Earth. Their population continued to drop. As of 2023,

Scientists say that without more protections, North Atlantic right whales could become extinct by 2040.

they are among the most endangered species of whales in the world. The species is very close to extinction. But Philip Hamilton, a scientist at the New England Aquarium, explains that there is still hope. He says, "This species can recover if we stop injuring and killing them."[2]

2

SEI WHALES

The sei whale is the third largest whale species. Females can grow up to 60 feet (18 m) long, while males are slightly smaller. The sei whale has a blue-gray or black upper body. On its back is a hooked fin. The sei whale uses baleen plates to eat. It feeds on crustaceans, squid, and fish.

Scientists estimate there are about 80,000 sei whales around the world. Sei whales are not easy to count, though. It's hard to see a sei whale well enough to recognize it. They don't breach the water often. Even when they dive, they don't rise

The average sei whale eats about 2,000 pounds (900 kg) of food every day.

out of the water the way other whales do. They simply sink below the surface.

Sei whales are hard to find. They move around a lot. One area may have sei whales for a while, but then the animals might disappear for years. The lack of knowledge about sei whales makes conservation more difficult.

SEI WHALES AND WHALING

Before the 1900s, whalers didn't kill many sei whales. Whalers preferred hunting blue whales and fin whales, the two largest kinds of whales. But by the middle of the

Sei whales can weigh up to 100,000 pounds (45,000 kg).

1900s, populations of blue whales and fin whales had dropped very low. Whalers began hunting sei whales on a large scale. By the time the IWC banned all commercial whaling, whalers may have killed about 300,000 sei whales.

GIANTS OF THE DEEP

Blue Whales: Up to 110 feet (34 m) long

Sei Whales: Up to 60 feet (18 m) long

North Atlantic Right Whales: Up to 52 feet (16 m) long

Gray Whales: Up to 49 feet (15 m) long

School Buses: Up to 35 feet (11 m) long

Sources: Cat Carrol, "How Long Is a School Bus?" Trail and Summit, n.d. https://trailandsummit.com.
"Species Directory," NOAA Fisheries, n.d. https://iwc.int.

Whales come in many different sizes.

Some countries weren't happy with the ban. Japan voted against it. When the ban came into force, Japan found a way to continue whaling.

The IWC still allowed whaling for scientific research. Countries could give scientists permits to kill the animals. The Japanese government allowed and supported scientific whaling. Many whalers sold the meat for people to eat. Some of the meat even ended up in school lunches. In 2004, Japanese whalers started catching one hundred sei whales in the North Pacific every year.

Conservation groups complained. They argued that Japan's whaling was commercial, not scientific. Greg Hunt, an Australian official, said, "There is no need to kill whales in the name of research."[3] He pointed out that scientists

ABORIGINAL WHALING

The IWC permits native, or aboriginal, whaling. The IWC recognizes that hunting whales to supply a community with whale products is different from killing large numbers of whales for profit. The IWC allows native communities in the United States, Russia, Greenland, and Saint Vincent and the Grenadines to hold whale hunts.

have more effective ways to study the creatures. In 2014, the United Nations' highest court ruled that Japan had to stop scientific whaling.

Japan tried to convince the IWC to allow commercial whaling. The IWC refused. In 2019, Japan responded by leaving the group. This meant the country no longer had to follow the ban. That summer, Japan allowed commercial whaling within the ocean waters it controlled. The government limited large-scale hunting to three whale species. Sei whales were among the three.

CURRENT THREATS

Some conservationists fear for the Western Coastal population of sei whales, the group of whales near Japan. Conservationists point out the Western Coastal population includes only about 400 sei whales. Other conservationists are just happy that Japan stopped whaling in other parts of the world, such as in the waters around Antarctica.

Commercial whaling may not last. Whaling is expensive. It also doesn't make much money. Whale meat isn't popular, especially with younger Japanese people. The government has to pay to

Other than humans, orcas are the sei whale's only predators.

keep the whaling industry going. In 2018, Japanese whaling cost $15 million more than it earned.

Patrick Ramage is a director at the International Fund for Animal Welfare.

Ramage believes Japan should lead the world in whale conservation, not in whaling. "Putting a dying industry on life support [and] killing more whales . . . are not steps in the right direction," Ramage says.[4]

Scientists continue to study sei whale populations. Conservationists keep fighting for the animals. They work on ways to reduce the dangers of ship strikes and fishing gear. Fortunately, scientists think sei whale numbers are increasing. If so, the species might not be considered endangered for long. But scientists can't be sure what's happening to the sei

Scientists can identify sei whales by their distinctive hooked fins.

whale population. The whales are hard to study. And even if they are taken off the endangered species list, the animals could remain at risk of becoming endangered once again.

3

BLUE WHALES

Blue whales are the largest species of whale. They are also the largest animals ever to live on Earth. Scientists think the whales are larger than any dinosaur. Some blue whales can grow up to 110 feet (34 m) long. They can weigh 330,000 pounds (150,000 kg).

Blue whale hearts are the size of a small car. Their tongues weigh about as much as an elephant.

Blue whales are long and thin. The tops of their bodies are blue-gray with light gray spots. They have small fins near their tails. These enormous animals can make very loud sounds. Other whales can hear them

Blue whales are among the loudest animals on the planet. They use their voices to communicate with other whales and to navigate.

from up to 1,000 miles (1,600 km) away. The animals can live eighty or ninety years.

Blue whales mostly eat krill. Krill look similar to shrimp. Krill form huge swarms in the open ocean. Blue whales rapidly turn, roll, and dive as they scoop up water full of krill. Afterward, they trap the krill with their baleen plates. A single blue whale can eat about 35,300 pounds (16,000 kg) of krill in a day.

BLUE WHALE POPULATIONS

Early whalers had trouble catching blue whales. The whales were too fast and big.

Blue whales were popular prey for whalers. A single whale could provide 120 barrels of whale oil.

But by the 1900s, whalers had invented new methods of hunting. Their ships were fast enough to catch up with the giants. New cannons shot exploding **harpoons**.

Huge factory ships could process a whole whale at sea. Whalers killed about 320,000 blue whales before the ban on commercial whaling.

Blue whale populations have risen since then. There are about 10,000 to 25,000 blue whales in the world. They live in all oceans except the Arctic Ocean. Different subspecies are found in different areas. A subspecies is a group within a species. Some blue whale subspecies are rare, such as the Antarctic subspecies. Scientists estimate that the Antarctic population is less than 1 percent of its pre-whaling size.

THREATS TO KRILL

Blue whales face many threats. One is related to their food source. In the Southern Ocean, the krill population has dropped significantly since the 1980s. This is dangerous for blue whales. They need to eat krill to survive.

AGING A WHALE

It's difficult to know a whale's age. Size can help scientists estimate age. Scientists can also use a dart to get a tiny bit of the animal to run tests on. If a whale dies, scientists can look at its teeth or earwax. Both have layers that mark each year, similar to the rings of a tree trunk.

Scientists think the loss of whales may play a part in the drop in krill populations. Whale poop puts a lot of **nutrients** into the water. Fewer nutrients in the water mean fewer nutrients for krill.

Climate change may also be killing krill. Near Antarctica, sea ice protects krill from predators and extreme weather. Warmer temperatures lead to less sea ice. That might lead to fewer krill. Climate change is also making the water more acidic. This makes it harder for krill to hatch.

Humans are also lowering the krill population. People harvest krill from

A blue whale eats about 40 million krill every day.

the wild. The crustaceans and their oil are rich in nutrients. Krill products can be used in medicine. People also use krill to feed fish.

Krill are very important to life in Antarctica. They provide food for many animals. Fish, squid, and seals eat krill. Seabirds such as penguins do too. Fewer krill could cause problems for all of these species.

OTHER DANGERS

Humans aren't the only creatures who hunt blue whales. Orcas, otherwise known as killer whales, go after these giants. Orcas are predators. Their diet includes fish, seabirds, sea lions, and whales. Orcas are found all over the world.

Orcas are much smaller than blue whales. The largest orcas reach only

32 feet (9.8 m) long. However, orcas hunt in groups. Fifty or more orcas working together can kill a blue whale. They often target smaller or younger ones.

Orca attacks are rare. But human threats are much more common. One poorly understood risk is pollution. Tiny bits of plastic called microplastics pollute

IDENTIFYING A WHALE

Scientists can tell each blue whale apart. Each whale's fin is as unique as a human fingerprint. Each whale also has its own pattern of light-gray spots. Identifying whales helps scientists better understand how many whales there are and how the animals are doing.

the ocean. Scientists think a single blue whale might eat 10 million pieces of microplastics every day. That adds up to 95 pounds (43 kg) of plastic each day.

"These numbers are huge," says scientist Matthew Savoca. "Of course, the animals themselves are also huge."[5] Savoca says scientists aren't sure if or how the microplastics harm the whales. But larger pieces of plastic can cause a lot of harm. They can cut the inside of a whale. The plastic can also fill the animal's stomach.

Like other endangered whales, blue whales are harmed and killed by

More whales may be killed by ships than researchers know. Experts estimate that only about 2 percent of blue whale ship strikes are reported.

fishing gear. Others die from ship strikes. The risk may be worst south of the island nation of Sri Lanka. This area is busy with shipping boats. Despite these threats, some populations of blue whales appear to be increasing.

4

GRAY WHALES

Before whaling, gray whales were common in northern oceans around the world. Now gray whales live mainly in the North Pacific. However, the western North Pacific population is endangered.

Gray whales grow up to 49 feet (15 m) long. Adults weigh around

99,000 pounds (45,000 kg). The whales start out dark gray. They turn lighter gray as adults. Their flippers are broad and pointed. The whales have a hump on their backs. Their backs are bumpy. The oldest known gray whale reached around seventy-five to eighty years of age.

Baby gray whales learn how to swim within thirty minutes of being born.

Gray whales live near coasts. Like other baleen whales, gray whales mostly feed on small crustaceans. They prefer feeding on the sea floor. First they roll onto their sides. Then they suck in mud as they swim. The whales push the mud and water out through their baleen plates and eat the crustaceans left behind.

Gray whales have one of the longest migrations of any animal. The whales travel from wintering grounds in the south to summer feeding grounds in the north. They may travel more than 12,000 miles (19,000 km) in a year.

Gray whales normally live alone or in small groups, but during migrations they travel in larger pods.

GRAY WHALE HISTORY

Gray whales were popular prey for whalers.

The whales stick to shallow waters

near coasts. This made them easier to find.

By the 1700s, whalers had driven gray

whales to extinction in the North Atlantic. Pacific gray whales were nearly extinct too. The ban on whaling helped the species survive.

Today, gray whales live in two populations. The larger population is found mostly along the west coast of North America. This group has been able to recover. In 1994, officials decided this population was no longer endangered. However, the animals still face threats. Between 2016 and 2022, their population dropped from about 27,000 to around 16,650.

Gray whales were hunted to create a variety of products. Their parts were used in makeup, food, chemicals, clothes, and more.

During the 1990s, scientists discovered a population of gray whales off the coast of Russia. This second population is much smaller. It has fewer than 300 gray whales. This population, called the western North Pacific population, is endangered.

THREATS TODAY

Orcas appear to be the main natural killers of gray whales. Other dangers come from human activities. Ship strikes can kill gray whales. The danger is especially high during migration. But scientists don't fully understand how bad the problem is. "The number of strikes of gray whales may range from the tens to low hundreds every year," says Gregory Silber, a scientist with Smultea Environmental Sciences.[6]

In 2019, increased numbers of dead gray whales began washing up on shore. These are called strandings. "There is no one

When certain chemicals enter the ocean, they poison gray whales. This can make it harder for the whales to have babies. It may also shorten their life spans.

thing that we can point to that explains all of the strandings," says Deborah Fauquier, a veterinarian with NOAA Fisheries.[7] Some of the dead whales had been struck by ships. Many appeared to be starving.

Climate change is likely one cause of the population drop. Most gray whales feed in seas far to the north. Climate change has been harming these regions. Changes in sea ice and water temperatures may be killing whale prey.

A big threat to the western population comes from the oil and gas industry. Some of the whales' western feeding grounds are above a gas field. Companies use loud sounds to find gas underground. The companies build platforms out on the water. The platforms are used to drill for gas. The sounds and platforms can disturb

Organizations such as the World Wildlife Fund are fighting to stop energy companies from harming gray whale habitats.

gray whales. Conservationists are trying to help. They're working with oil and gas companies to find ways to protect whales.

GRAY WHALES TODAY

Gray whales are popular with whale watchers because of their behavior.

The animals are curious about boats. Sometimes they raise their heads out of the water. This behavior is called spy hopping. They also often leap partway out of the water. This is called breaching.

Unfortunately, whale watching can cause problems. The boats can bother gray whales. Whale watching can make the whales leave their feeding areas. Whale-watching ships can accidentally hit whales. But whale watching also gives people the chance to appreciate these ocean giants up close. It can encourage people to support whale conservation.

The ban on commercial whaling helped many whale species. Some have recovered. In 2016, most humpback whales were no longer considered endangered. One population of gray whales has bounced back. The future of other endangered whale species depends on the conservation measures people put in place.

WHALE WATCHING

Whale watching began in the 1950s. A California man charged people a dollar to see gray whales from his boat. In 2009, the industry brought in $2.1 billion around the world. More than 13 million people took part. Other popular whale-watching species include blue whales, humpback whales, and minke whales.

GLOSSARY

climate change
shifts in temperature and weather related to global warming caused by human activities

commercial
related to making a profit

conservation
the act of protecting or preserving wildlife

crustaceans
a group of animals with hard outsides and no backbones, such as crabs and shrimp

extinct
no longer existing

harpoons
weapons similar to spears that are attached to a long line and used for catching large sea creatures

migrate
to move from one area to another at a certain time of year

nutrients
chemicals in food that living things need in order to survive and grow

SOURCE NOTES

CHAPTER ONE: NORTH ATLANTIC RIGHT WHALES

1. "North Atlantic Right Whale," *NOAA Fisheries*, November 7, 2022. www.fisheries.noaa.gov.

2. Quoted in Cliff White, "USA—Around 340 North Atlantic Right Whales Remaining as Population Continues to Decline," *Coastal News Today*, October 25, 2022. www.coastalnewstoday.com.

CHAPTER TWO: SEI WHALES

3. Quoted in Justin McCurry, "Japanese Whaling Fleet to Set Sail for Antarctica," *Guardian*, November 30, 2015. www.theguardian.com.

4. Quoted in "Japan's Killing of 25 Endangered Whales Is Unsustainable and Indefensible," *International Fund for Animal Welfare*, November 12, 2021. www.ifaw.org.

CHAPTER THREE: BLUE WHALES

5. Quoted in Madeleine Cuff, "Blue Whales Could Be Eating 10 Million Pieces of Plastic Every Day," *New Scientist*, November 1, 2022. www.newscientist.com.

CHAPTER FOUR: GRAY WHALES

6. Quoted in "New IUCN-Backed Study Finds Gray Whales at High Risk from Ship Strikes in the North Pacific Ocean," *IUCN*, February 26, 2021. www.iucn.org.

7. Quoted in Maya Yang, "North American Gray Whale Counts Dwindling for the Last Two Years," *Guardian*, October 9, 2022. www.theguardian.com.

FOR FURTHER RESEARCH

BOOKS

Mark Carwardine, *Handbook of Whales, Dolphins, and Porpoises of the World*. Princeton, NJ: Princeton University Press, 2020.

Kelly Gauthier, *Discovering Whales, Dolphins and Porpoises: The Ultimate Guide to the Ocean's Largest Mammals*. New York: Applesauce Press, 2020.

Brian Skerry, *Secrets of the Whales*. Washington, DC: National Geographic, 2021.

INTERNET SOURCES

"Blue Whale," *World Wildlife Fund*, n.d. www.worldwildlife.org.

"How Big Is the Biggest Whale?" *Wonderopolis*, n.d. www.wonderopolis.org.

"Whale," *San Diego Zoo Wildlife Alliance: Animals and Plants*, n.d. https://animals.sandiegozoo.org.

WEBSITES

Discovery of Sound in the Sea
https://dosits.org

Discovery of Sound in the Sea is an interactive website run by the University of Rhode Island. The site allows users to listen to the sounds made by different marine animals, including several species of baleen whales.

DK FindOut!: Whales, Dolphins, and Porpoises
https://www.dkfindout.com/us/animals-and-nature/whales-dolphins-and-porpoises

DK FindOut! hosts videos, articles, and interactive activities about a variety of interesting subjects. Its "Whales, Dolphins, and Porpoises" page lets readers learn more about whales and other marine mammals.

Ocean Alliance
https://whale.org

Founded in 1971, Ocean Alliance works to protect whales and their habitats. The group works to teach people how to care for the world's oceans. The website contains information about whales, the dangers facing the creatures, and how to protect them.

INDEX

aboriginal groups, 28
Antarctica, 30, 38, 40–41
Arctic Ocean, 38

baleen, 11–12, 22, 36, 48
blubber, 16
blue whales, 19, 24–25, 26, 34–45, 57
breaching, 23, 56

calves, 13, 17
coloring, 10, 22, 35, 43, 47

fin whales, 19, 24–25
fins, 22, 35, 43
fishing gear, 6–8, 15, 16–17, 20, 32, 44–45
flippers, 10, 47

global warming, 40, 54
gray whales, 26, 46–57

heads, 10, 56
humpback whales, 19, 57

International Whaling Commission, 8–9, 25, 27–29

Japan, 27–32

krill, 36, 39–42

life span, 10, 36, 39, 47

microplastics, 43–44
migrations, 13, 48–49, 52
minke whales, 57

National Oceanic and Atmospheric Administration, 13, 53
noise pollution, 17, 54–55
North Atlantic right whales, 6–8, 10–21, 26
North Pacific right whales, 19

orcas, 42–43, 52

populations, 8, 15, 20, 22, 30, 32–33, 38, 39–40, 45, 50, 51, 57
prey, 12, 22, 36, 39–42, 48, 54

Russia, 28, 51

sei whales, 22–33
ship strikes, 15, 18–20, 32, 45, 52
size, 22, 26, 34–35, 43, 46–47
strandings, 52–53

tails, 10, 35

United Nations, 29
United States, 13, 18, 28

whale meat, 8, 27, 30
whale sounds, 19, 35–36
whale watching, 55–56, 57
whaling, 8–9, 13–15, 16, 24–32, 36–38, 42, 46, 49–50, 57

IMAGE CREDITS

Cover: © Foto4440/iStockphoto

5: © doescher/iStockphoto

7: © Florida Fish and Wildlife Conservation Commission/NOAA

9: © NOAA

11: © NOAA Fisheries/NOAA

12: © NOAA

14: © Sea to Shore Alliance/NOAA

21: © NOAA

23: © Gerard Soury/The Image Bank/Getty Images

25: © Doug Perrine/Blue Planet Archive

26 (whales): © pixorena/Shutterstock Images

26 (bus): © Denis Dubrovin/Shutterstock Images

31: © slowmotiongli/Shutterstock Images

33: © Ellen O'Donnell/NOAA Teacher at Sea Program/NOAA

35: © Alex Mustard/Nature Picture Library/Alamy

37: © Raymond M. Gilmore/NOAA Central Library Historical Fisheries Collection/ NOAA

41: © Apple Pho/Shutterstock Images

45: © Andrew Sutton/Shutterstock Images

47: © Travis Potter/Shutterstock Images

49: © slowmotiongli/iStockphoto

51: © Joe Morris 917/Shutterstock Images

53: © Mogens Trolle/Shutterstock Images

55: © SINCHAI_B/Shutterstock Images

ABOUT THE AUTHOR

Clara MacCarald is a freelance writer with a master's degree in ecology and natural resources. She lives with her family in an off-grid house nestled in the forests of central New York. When not parenting her daughter, she spends her time writing nonfiction books for kids.